To Val,
love
Mona Joseph

Chancing Life
Wisdom in a Dice Toss

By
Mona Van Joseph

This work is an original method of divination. Though the answers provided in this book are compelling, you possess free will and you are ultimately responsible for the quality of your life. The author and affiliated organizations are not responsible for your decisions, choices or actions.

The melody that enriches the woman:

Chuck

Grateful thanks to **Steve Bornfeld**
for his editing assistance.

And to **Amber Mayes**
for cover design, book format and layout.

Introduction

I believe there are no accidents and that everything has a purpose in life. To some people that may seem naive, but I would rather think that fortunate and unfortunate things happen for a reason. Having stated that, let's think for the time being that we live in a benevolent Universe. Many intricate elements had to be right for humans to even exist, and it's truly a miracle that we do. You were created to bring your unique gift to the world and your environment continues to support your journey.

I am offering you a simple way to connect with the divine plan you chose for yourself before deciding to be born in this lifetime. I believe everyone significant in our life was chosen by us as a catalyst to learn the lessons we are here to learn. We chose our parents, our siblings, our lovers, our spouses, our friends, our children, and our enemies. Each soul we connect with brings us exactly the lesson we are supposed to learn at the precise moment we need to learn it. The Universe is always working for our greatest benefit.

Your grandmother may have read the tea leaves at the bottom of her cup to predict her day ahead, or your favorite aunt looked into your palm for your potential. Learning to pay attention to signs and omens as our ancestors recognized them was how we made sense of the world. Whatever the method, the results allowed us the poise to prepare for any upcoming experience.

I offer the simple toss of two dice. The 36 combinations can be used for meditation, or maybe for you to consider a fresh perspective on an issue. You may look to address a specific question or a general lesson of the day, and this method offers you a different focus.

The answers in this method of divination can be compelling, however, since you have free will, any choice, action, or decision, is entirely your responsibility.

This book is dedicated to those people who look to allow their truest self to manifest in their lives and bring them the love, abundance, and joy they deserve. Learn to enjoy the miracle of all things, for it is my blessing to you and your birthright.

Mona

TABLE OF CONTENTS

TABLE OF CONTENTS (cont.)

Chapter One

Imagine that you are a perfect spirit of light and love. Before your incarnation into this lifetime, that's exactly who you are - omnipotent, glorious and perfect. This is your Higher Self, the Self of all things. You made the decision to embrace this human experience (as the human self); you selected the personality and physical form that would best suit the lessons chosen. The limited human self does not easily recognize the power and energy available.

During times of stress we can accomplish great things because we move past fear and into action. We allow that action because we have a reason (perhaps protecting someone we love or an "emergency") to act bravely. Think instead, that you already have the permission to pursue your greatest goals. This guidebook will help you recognize that the Universe is always working for you, not against you. When you cast the dice for an answer – you are seeking a perspective that is already a part of you. If you can form the question, you can know the answer.

We are not at the mercy of some whim or destiny that is beyond or outside of us. We are simply aligning our self with the path we chose to embrace before the incarnation of this lifetime. This puts the power where it belongs - our perfect enlightened spirit directing our mundane human self.

This concept is especially powerful when we witness something that began in us as a thought and then manifests into our outward reality. This is the power of "I". I choose, I am, and I exist. That's what makes this life so magical, the power of our choices, the power of self-awareness, and the gift of this life. If we were supposed to live our lives for the sake of others, then why were we all born with differences? Why is it we are not a school of minnows moving in unison for no real purpose except movement, food, safety, and procreation? We are not beings born to exclusively serve – we are born to realize that we exist to become our highest potential. You are no good to yourself (or anyone else) if you ignore your true identity. Your true self is connected with the Divine and can accomplish astonishing goals.

When you speak of "I" it is the unique aspect, impression, and gift that acknowledges Self. When thought or spoken, the word "I" is what touches our essence of life and represents our unique gift of expression in this world. This is not selfish but self-aware. You must have a strong sense of yourself as who you really are before you can make any sense of your destiny and purpose. Once we reach our age of reason (and that varies for each person) it is essential that you decide for yourself what your gift is. It is not what your peers or authority figures taught you (or expected of you), it is your sense of your talents and what you know in the deepest part of your soul to be your quest. You may have the intelligence to become a physicist but not the desire. There is a clue here however: what you love is usually what you hold talent for and that is the first step into reaching your personal destiny. True happiness and contentment in life is about how much you love, not how many people love you. What you love is what defines you.

Just opening your mind to the possibility that you have more influence than you think will start the process of truly embracing this life and your potential. It is both empowering and frightening to be yourself. Most people are the sum total of others' opinions of them. While it is nice to hear the positive (and otherwise the negative) allowing others to have too much influence on our sense of self by their opinions never serves us. Living up to your own expectations is always more difficult than living up to someone else's. This is especially significant if a parent who never followed their dream reared you.

Regardless of your upbringing, your spirit chose this life and the situation in which you are living it to best suit why you are here. If your childhood was far from "normal" it was for you to have the gift of that personal perspective and do something with it or about it. At some point, we are supposed to acknowledge our power and potential. When you begin to treat your life as a choice and not as a victim, then you have taken the first step toward your providence.

When you cast the dice you are engaging the best of yourself. You are beginning to trust yourself and your capacity. It is now time to give your Self the permission to shine. I choose, I am, I exist, I love, and I live.

Chapter Two

The Dice

The best dice to purchase for the castings described in this workbook are the ones used in a casino. Those dice have been specially balanced to produce the most random result. You may purchase your dice at quality gaming companies or pick up a pair on your next trip to your favorite casino. It does not matter if the dice have been tossed previously and then retired to the gift shop.

When you get your dice home, I recommend this simple cleansing ritual to designate them specifically for your castings. Take a small bowl and sprinkle a thin layer of sea salt or kosher salt inside the bottom. Place your new dice on top of the salt at the bottom of the bowl. Pour salt over the dice until they are buried. Leave them for 24 hours in the salt. After 24 hours, remove the dice from the salt. Your dice are now ready for use.

There is space provided for you at the end of each chapter to record your question with each dice combination. Tracking the dice castings will assist you in recognizing patterns that may repeat within a short period of time. You may use this method to ask a variety of questions or simply to ask what is the most important lesson of the day. You will notice many answers connected with each number combination. A key word*, a simple "yes" or "no" answer, and an in-depth meaning are provided for each combination.

The purpose of this method of divination is to help you recognize that the Universe always is working for you and the visual example can be meaningful and supportive. Each combination will have a suggested affirmation for you to consider. Writing this affirmation on a small piece of paper and carrying it with you for the day will help you with focus and awareness. The more you use this method, the more you'll notice your life becoming calmer and more purposeful.

Prepare the environment where your dice will be cast. A shallow wooden box that is typically used to hold papers works well when it is lined with a soft, plain material. The color of the material is not important, as long as it is pattern-free.

The best time of day to consult the dice for meditation is in the morning, however, you may cast the dice at any time if you have a specific question. Hold the dice in your left hand and consider the question or issue with which you are seeking guidance. Imagine that the exact answer you need at that moment will present itself. Or, simply think about the most important thing you need to know right now and allow the dice to present your lesson of the moment. Simply focus on the question and allow the dice to fall from your hand.

Once the dice have rolled from your hand, whichever one seems more to the left is read as the first number of the combination. If you roll a vertical pattern, read the upper dice as the first number. There is a difference in this method of divination between rolling a three and five or rolling a five and three. Each meaning is number and order specific. You may also choose to roll the dice individually so you know which dice is to be read first.

Look up the meaning of your combination in the following chapters. The first number is your perspective in the situation and the second is the lesson. The combination of both dice produces the answer to your question. "Yes" and "no" answers are provided for those questions in which that answer is appropriate. You may use the dice in a past, present, and future manner about a specific situation by rolling them three times. First roll represents past, second the present, and third the future.

Because we always have the power of choice, your will is always the overruling aspect in any situation. Remember, you are always the one in control and nothing happens in your life until you decide. Watch what happens when you choose to engage your world. Take a chance and roll the dice. You deserve the best that you can possibly imagine.

*Key word and dice combination list is provided in Appendix.

Chancing Life

ONE

The beginning of all things and parallel to the word "I."
It is who we are and the sum of our choices directly
related to our gifts and expression on this Earth plane.

One is your identity.

ONE + ONE
DIVINE AGREEMENT
(supporting gem/mineral: gold)

YES

Physical Plane:

Casting ONE + ONE predicts that the solution to your problem will arrive by your attentiveness to others. For the next week, treat each individual you meet as if they have the answer to your question. You will not have to ask for help, nor even ask your question, it will present itself to you in the proper form at the proper time.

We are all here on Earth to help each other reach our greatest potential. This is not a position of servitude; rather, it is one of recognizing the spiritual guides that manifest to us as fellow humans. Simply by waiting for the answer to unfold through another will place your mind in the attitude of receptivity.

Keep your secrets and wait for the answer.

Spiritual Perspective:

This is the divine agreement between you and your higher self. Your spirit chose this moment in time to exist. You chose what your body looks like; your family, significant loves; how smart you are; and the meaningful relationships you attract in this lifetime. Your spirit chose to manifest for a specific purpose and your quest in this life-time is to achieve your highest potential.

You chose all the people that presented significant challenges and it is always about learning the importance of this moment. Learn and then release. Be especially attentive to people who have nothing to gain regarding your issue. The older you are, the more you have accomplished, even though it may not seem that way. You are exactly the person you are for the purpose of this lifetime.

This is also the balance of the masculine and the feminine within you. If you find that those scales are imbalanced, it's time to make the appropriate adjustments. If you've been constantly questing after a goal, consider shifting your perspective to one of patience and waiting. Or, you might want to become more dynamic if you have been thinking that the goal will arrive with little effort on your part.

Our greatest desires materialize out of just being aware of the potential of the moment.

Ritual:

Write your question on a small slip of paper with the following affirmation: "The answer to my question now manifests for the benefit of all concerned."

ONE + TWO
GATHERING
(supporting gem/mineral: yellow topaz)

NO

Physical Plane:

Casting ONE + TWO indicates that you don't have enough information to make this decision or take action. There are still secrets that are being withheld from you and it is a good idea to postpone your commitment until such time that important information is gathered. This question always includes other people. All doubts about this next step must be answered before you will know if this is the right move to make. If you are deciding about a new career opportunity, make sure you know all about the company you are considering. If you have asked about a relationship, there are still unanswered concerns. This is a time of inquiry not action.

Form the most enlightening questions and then inquire.

Spiritual Perspective:

Take the time to consider your life path. You are amazingly powerful and others are recognizing your strength. This is a time in your life where opportunities are presenting themselves more quickly because you have established your potential for a meaningful partnership, career advancement, or beginning any project on your own.

Do not expend resources or be impulsive at this time. Be cheerful and optimistic that the appropriate information will unfold at the exact moment for you to make this decision. You are mature enough spiritually to handle the situation presented to you, but on a soul level you are not willing to sacrifice the time if the decision does not serve your highest potential.

You are at a point in your life where time is your most important commodity; nothing should waste this precious gift. Anything on which you choose to bestow your attention needs to be of appropriate value. This question is about preparing your turning point in this life. You are on the brink of desired changes; make sure that you are serving your best interest.

Sometimes hesitancy is a gift from our Self.

Ritual:

On a small slip of paper write the following affirmation: "The value of my time is appropriately rewarded."

ONE + THREE
PRIORITIES
(supporting gem/mineral: moldavite)

YES

Physical Plane:

Casting ONE + THREE embraces material desires and is about bringing "things" into your life. It is about learning to focus your mind on a specific possession or situation. Are you seeking wealth for a more comfortable lifestyle? Are you looking to move to a new physical environment? Do you want a new car? You may have anything you want once you focus on that goal. There is nothing wrong with wanting possessions that you enjoy. It allows comfort, safety, and a reflection of confidence that you can create anything you wish in this lifetime.

Decide on what you want and then plan to have it.

Spiritual Perspective:

Every "thing" in this world began as a thought. That knowledge can draw to you any material possession, any job situation, or great love. This allows you to live in an attitude of abundance. When you really desire something, behaving as if it is already an aspect of your life (or on its way) allows you the ability to release emotional anticipation.

Some people live in the perspective that wanting material things in life is somehow evil or greedy. It's envy that is evil. Thinking that you are "less-than" because you don't have the most perfect nose, or drive the biggest car cuts off the abundance mindset. Once you decide that you can have anything you want just by simple focus, it allows you to celebrate and appreciate that others have achieved abundance in their lifetime. This recognition of potential embraces the natural right to reflect the abundant capacity of each being.

The environment around you, your material possessions, and your living space, are a clear indication of your spiritual and mental clarity. People with this clarity celebrate material wealth. They enjoy and acknowledge this abundance, but they also know that these accessories are temporary. This detachment to the "things" costs little emotional expense because they know possessions can be repeatedly created.

Embrace that your Self knows only abundance.

Ritual:

Write down on paper the thing you desire with the following affirmation: "This or something better manifests for me and the benefit of all concerned."

ONE + FOUR
FOUNDATION

(supporting gem/mineral: black tourmaline)

NO

Physical Plane:

Casting ONE + FOUR is about planning and structure. Check that every financial, material, and physical item is working in accord to your question. This is about the tedious task of checking all the details. Make sure the financing, people, and materials required for the question are available. This is about selfishly making sure that all aspects of the project are working on your behalf. This is not a good time for assumption of capacity and ability. You are personally required to perform this "checking," as it will truly affect you.

You must first care for yourself before you can care for anything else.

Spiritual Perspective:

Defining what is important to you is the first step in creating an authentic sense of self. This is about living up to your own potential and expectations. It is actually easier to live up to another's idea of success and accomplishment because you do not have to decide for yourself what's important.

We have been taught that selfishness is distasteful, but it is those with a strong sense of self that have accomplished the greatest things in their lifetime. They are not trying to live up to their mother or father's expectations – they are living up to their own. That is a much more difficult concept to initially grasp because it means that you will probably have to change your "foundation" or support system in some way.

Your perspective and potential are unique to you and therefore, are the individual expression of the Divine within you. Trust that you know the right thing to do and you will know how to handle any challenge or opportunity that presents itself. You are no good to yourself or anyone else if you have not decided how you will live your life from this point forward.

Your recognition of Self is the most liberating viewpoint.

Ritual:

Write down on a slip of paper the following affirmation: "Each event moves me closer to the recognition of my highest potential."

ONE + FIVE
INTENTION
(supporting gem/mineral: citrine)

YES

Physical Plane:

The combination of ONE + FIVE is about advertising what you want. Tell everyone who has the potential to help you about your intentions. If you are seeking a loving companion, a new job, a vacation, or a material thing, this is the time to talk about your objective. Do not be shy; this is about you expanding your circle to bring you what you know in your heart you may have. Contact people from the past, communicate your goals and then allow those goals to materialize. Write down what you want, place it in an envelope, seal it and put it on your refrigerator with a magnet.

Form a clear picture of what you want and talk about it.

Spiritual Perspective:

Allowing yourself permission to create what you want is the way to bring forth a fulfilling life. You will eventually teach others the way to fashion their own goals and desires. By the experience of manifesting your desires, you can easily set an example of how to work with the flow of all things. There are no accidents and pure intent on your part allows the Universe to direct to you exactly what you require.

If you are emphasizing "lack" in your life, then that is what you will receive. If you do not think there's enough, then that is what you will experience. Operate from the perspective of abundance and that will bring observable and measurable results. You will find that the person or thing will find its way to you with very little effort on your part. Your poise will be one of awareness and then the energy to take action when the appropriate omen occurs.

Clear intention allows you flexibility and the ability to adapt to rapid changes. The more disruptive the flow of events, the more your current perspective or environment was not working toward your best possible potential. Embrace that this discomfort is actually moving you toward your right of abundance.

Pure intent produces beneficial results.

Ritual:

Write down on a piece of paper the following affirmation: "Each personal interaction brings my goal closer to me and I will recognize the appropriate moment to act."

ONE + SIX
RELEASE
(supporting gem/mineral: topaz)

NO

Physical Plane:

Casting ONE + SIX is about releasing the past. You cannot achieve the goal of your question until you do so. Usually this casting represents a former love relationship that was not resolved and painful hurt feelings still linger. This is the time to release and forgive that person or situation for not being what you expected at that point in your life. The quicker you liberate yourself from the cloud of the past, the more efficient you become in embracing the new and more empowering aspects of your life. Write about the past struggle that holds you back and then go outside and burn the words.

The past no longer applies to you.

Spiritual Perspective:

Other people, though well intentioned, may have colored your perspective with doubt about your abilities and value. This can be a reflection of an internal insecure view or, more likely, it may be that it is exactly the reason you created that past interaction in the first place. We are on Earth to learn lessons and reach our highest potential, so it makes sense that each situation would actually benefit us in some way.

You are in exactly the situation you need to be in for each lesson learned. Whichever event was triggered in your mind when you consulted the dice, it is exactly the correct one for you to examine. Listen for words of limitation that are not your own. If the words are not yours, then you need to forgive that person and instead embrace that they have provoked you to embrace a potentially more gratifying perspective.

Use any anger or hurt to motivate you toward your own happiness. Consider how your life would have been different (and maybe less fulfilling) if that "past" still existed today. If it was a great love, bless them for opening your heart, if it was a challenging work situation or business failure, bless the fact that you have knowledge of what did not prosper or benefit you.

The past prepares us to appreciate the prosperity and joy of now and the future.

Ritual:

Write down on a piece of paper the following affirmation: "All things presented to me recognize my current and future potential."

Date	Question

Date	Question

TWO

The partnering of all things and related to the word "We."
It is the people we choose to surround our destiny.
Others constantly assist us with our lessons and goals.

Two is our reflection.

TWO + ONE
GRATITUDE
(supporting gem/mineral: amber)

NO

Physical Plane:

The numbers TWO + ONE asks you to recognize those people along the way who have helped you achieve certain goals. These people may not be currently involved with your life but it is important that they be acknowledged. A simple thank you may suffice or perhaps you return a favor, in kind, at the level at which they assisted you. If they helped you with public recognition in some way, help them be recognized publicly. Maybe they introduced you to a meaningful person, so you introduce them to someone who is potentially meaningful.

Gratitude paves the way to a more significant and rewarding experience.

Spiritual Perspective:

Openly expressing your gratitude allows your heart and eyes to open to the perspective that the Universe is always working on our behalf. Recognizing the people that brought you to this moment in life creates natural goodwill. Even people who may have treated us badly in the past deserve at least mental recognition for the motivation they provided for our betterment.

You are the sum total of your self-motivation. The books you have read, the meaningful relationships, the teachers, and the enemies have all brought you to the perspective of this moment. It is time to pause and reflect on the contribution of others toward your success. If you think no one helped you to get to where you are then you have created a stalemate in your progress.

To begin movement in your life or career, it is important that the perspective of gratitude now flows through you. Practice genuine appreciation in even the smallest of tasks. Be especially thoughtful to people who serve you in some way. Go about your day with authentic thankfulness in your heart – it is time to realize how blessed you are. That will release the stagnant feeling in your life.

A grateful heart recognizes and embraces all things.

Ritual:

Write the following affirmation on a piece of paper: "I am grateful for all the wonderful assistance in my past, present, and future."

TWO + TWO
FRIENDSHIP
(supporting gem/mineral: emerald)

YES

Physical Plane:

TWO + TWO represents appreciating all friendships in this lifetime. This is an internal appreciation, not necessarily an external appreciation. It is now time to acknowledge the credibility of friendships without the conscious knowledge of the people considered. This is where you extend a favor or two behind the scenes on their behalf. You will find that by touting someone else's business, friendship, or good experience that more beneficial tidings find their way to you. This is a way to add more depth to your business, relationships or situations simply by recognizing greatness in others.

Sing the praises of someone you care about.

Spiritual Perspective:

Our best friends and most meaningful relationships reflect what we like about ourselves. By touting the wonderful things about others, you are actually talking about the things within you that you admire. The flip side of this exercise is true as well; if we do not appreciate something about another person, then we are considering aspects of our more negative nature.

Envy is the most destructive characteristic we can adopt. Immature spiritual development may appear as envy, especially when we find that we are repeatedly comparing our life to another's. When you admire someone for their accomplishments, then you allow your energy to be transformed from criticism to celebration. With this new attitude, the good things in life will find their way to you.

The most disarming way to deal with envy is to imagine that anything another can do we can do for ourselves. We all have something within us that is unique. It is up to us to embrace what we can contribute that brings us abundance and contentment. By complimenting the accomplishments of others you actually bring yourself greater approving energy by those around you.

Your atmosphere becomes one of thoughtful genuineness.

Ritual:

Write the following affirmation on a piece of paper: "I have all that I need to bring forth abundance and I admire those individuals who have achieved their goals in this lifetime."

TWO + THREE
UNITY

(supporting gem/mineral: obsidian)

NO

Physical Plane:

Rolling TWO + THREE denotes a meeting of some sort to decide the answer. There are other items or people to consider in relation to your question. These may be events that have not yet transpired. Either way, the timing is not right for you to move forward in action. A dedication or rededication to the outcome is called for now. The situation has become scattered and unfocused. A meeting with the people involved must be scheduled as soon as possible. You cannot do this project by yourself; there is support and assistance at your fingertips.

Unity of different skills brings success.

Spiritual Perspective:

Your commitment to the goal is the first part of the equation and that is firmly established in your mind. The challenge arises when you realize that the others involved may be actually undermining the project or goal because of unclear understanding. Important items must be presented in written form to all concerned to bring about success. You may have to direct people in a specific manner for visible results.

The people involved see the goal differently than you. In a way, you may have to go back to the beginning of the project and start again. Success is expected once everyone knows how to contribute. Start by having each person write down how they visualize the ultimate result. It will then allow you to know how to interact and engage the energies of each person.

Although you know success is imminent, the others involved do not embrace how it will ultimately benefit them. People cannot read your mind, and your challenge is to learn how to motivate others to help you achieve this goal. This is an important lesson to assist you in future success. Although you would like to delegate this task to someone else, you will receive more enthusiasm if you have people involved directly report to you.

Your direct influence will benefit others involved in greater ways than you expect.

Ritual:

Write the following affirmation on a slip of paper: "All individuals connected to this outcome work toward and achieve the highest possible success."

TWO + FOUR
KINDNESS
(supporting gem/mineral: garnet)

YES

Physical Plane:

TWO + FOUR suggests that even strangers offer some wisdom for your question. While engaging in everyday activities, treat each person as if they are the most important person of the moment. Today is the day to send money anonymously to a charity. Today is the day you talk to someone new and be very interested in what they have to tell you. This is the day you give the gift of attentiveness to everyone. You will only invest a moment longer than usual but it will begin an awareness within you that all things in this Universe support you.

Kindness to everyone today forms Universal support tomorrow.

Spiritual Perspective:

Recognizing the interconnection of all things is the surest way to personal enlightenment. Interaction with all the important and unimportant parts of your world will help you feel connected. The simple act of thanking someone for what you may consider a menial task allows you to respect the gifts of your life. This is where you acknowledge that you could not be at this point in life if it were not for the people in it.

Begin by displaying kindness to your parents; take a moment in silent meditation for the gift of your life in this world. This gratitude applies for whomever you consider a positive parent figure. For those who chose a more difficult path, thank and forgive those who have helped guide you to this point. Offer benevolence in your heart to those who were inconsiderate, awkward, or rude.

By filling your heart with the strength of a gentle sovereign, you will not experience fear. Others will recognize your power and embrace you in the same manner. We are all spiritual beings in human form; behaving in this manner allows us to ultimately believe our immortality. Realizing that our lessons often manifest through coincidental meetings, this kindness to the unknown keeps us in a perfect open-mind perspective.

Be prepared for the gifts that come to you just by being thoughtful.

Ritual:

Write down on the piece of paper the following affirmation: "The Universe will mirror all my best qualities."

TWO + FIVE
CREDIBLE WITNESS
(supporting gem/mineral: pyrite)

NO

Physical Plane:

Rolling TWO + FIVE implies self-examination through the eyes of others. Consider this a checkpoint for your progress. See what emotions are mirrored back to you today. This is the time of checking how others respond to you and your goals. Act on those encouraging words and meditate on what you resist hearing. Remember, everyone in your circle is here to assist you in becoming the most empowered being that you can conceive yourself to be. There is no loss of power; you are reserving it for the correct moment. This time is a small pause before meaningful action.

It is okay to examine your blind spot.

Spiritual Perspective:

All things around you reflect your inner perspective. If you maintain a clean and orderly house, then your mind is orderly and efficient. A cluttered environment at home or work distracts you from clear and productive focus. Today is the day to examine the material things around you as well as the people you attract. Because all things mirror our mind's potential, self-esteem and attitude, check and make sure you are sending the correct message to yourself and others.

The task of a total house cleansing* is more than just dusting. Real cleaning is removing the following items from your home: icons that remind you of depressing events from a past or current event; any item that is broken, doesn't fit, is not used, is spoiled; and anything representing death or decay. Removing plants that do not thrive and replacing them with plants that are healthy is a good way of changing energy.

This arduous task is also a way to change your luck and outlook. The most successful people have the most flowing and clear atmosphere. Surround yourself with the best environment you can create. If you feel comfortable and energized in that space then you have given yourself the best possible perspective for accomplishment. Your home, car, and office must be places that allow you a gratifying, empowering perspective.

Are you sending out a truthful message?

Ritual:

On a slip of paper write the following affirmation: "I create the ideal environment for success with my every action, word, and deed."

*See appendix for cleansing ritual.

TWO + SIX
SOUL MATE CONNECTION
(supporting gem/mineral: rose quartz)

YES

Physical Plane:

Casting TWO + SIX is about soul connections. This is about true love, deep, meaningful friendships, and the liberation that accompanies this level of companionship with another. Specifically, this is about celebrating or attracting one other person. If you have that person in your life, it is time to rejoice that you are creating something greater than you could have ever accomplished on your own. If you are seeking to incorporate great love in your life, manifested through a union with another, then now is the time that the Universe is blessing you with the tools to do so.

I am now willing to experience blissful love in my life.

Spiritual Perspective:

Surrendering our guard to great love is the most difficult barrier to dissolve. You will know the right person when he or she empowers you to feel greater than yourself. The most remarkable aspect of this attraction is that you want the same for them. This means you love this person enough to know that if at some point they require something beyond you to learn and grow as a spirit, you are willing to allow them to embrace that.

This is not a one-way street; that person wishes the same for you- loving this way keeps the relationship dynamic and fresh. We choose at a soul level that which will bring us the great joyful lessons in this lifetime with another being. When we find each other, there is no stress about how to behave, our outward appearance, or the level of material wealth. It is uncalculated and something beyond the rules of the world.

Soul connections exist for all aspects of life, and this combination may indicate a temptation of some magnitude. For those already married, the spiritual significance of temptation is to help you recognize that it is not the other person who will make your life more enhanced; it is the permission you have granted yourself to be more enhanced. In your current situation, it is your responsibility to bless and release all the emotions connected with this attraction.

You have all the joys of our greatest gift – the capacity to love.

Ritual:

On a slip of paper write the following affirmation: "I am the giver and receiver of great love."

Date	Question

Date	Question

THREE

Three is the number of spiritual connection in all things
and relates to the word "Creative."
This number reminds you that there are
infinite paths to all things.

Three represents divine inspiration and flow.

THREE + ONE
REFLECTION
(supporting gem/mineral: pearl)

YES

Physical Plane:

Producing THREE + ONE in your casting of the dice indicates that it is time to examine the past in regard to your question. How many times have you asked this question in your life? What results have you accomplished by doing things the same way? The desired outcome of your question will be achieved by embracing a new technique or experience. This combination is frequently produced when someone is repeating unfavorable patterns in their life. This is the time to radically change the manner in which you produce results.

Freeing yourself from past experience produces a favorable consequence.

Spiritual Perspective:

When we compare our experience to another, we subconsciously project stubbornness and a desire to continue to embrace a time from the past. It is a more powerful process to state that you possess the capability to tackle the current situation. This is not a time to brag about accomplishments or to believe that past education or experience provides you with the credentials to entitle you to something.

You would not be at this point in your life if you were not capable of allowing yourself this new opportunity. This is not about permission by another or proving to someone that you are attractive, worthy and capable. This is about shedding the past so you continue to learn. Be open and enthusiastic about this new direction. That will earn you more joy than anything from any time in your past.

This is about seeing the same world with new eyes. Sometimes, you will receive this combination at the time of abrupt change. Fear thrives in these times if you let it. Trust that you would not have arranged for this change to happen if your soul was not ready. Your spirit is ready to embrace a new way to live and love. The past way of living no longer applies to your new way of life.

Your potential has yet to be realized.

Ritual:

On a slip of paper write the following affirmation: "All my past has lead me to this moment of embracing my new way."

THREE + TWO
POTENTIAL

(supporting gem/mineral: opal)

NO

Physical Plane:

Casting THREE + TWO is about trying what you have never done before. It may be creating a new job; a new relationship; a new place of residence, or a new spiritual perspective. Usually when we become comfortable (complacent) and do not generate action, something will happen to force us take action in some direction. You may find that the job you once enjoyed gets uncomfortable, or that a supervisor becomes difficult in some way. A meaningful person in your life decides on a new direction that does not include you. Your life is about to change for the better even if that change is unsettling.

The bigger the change created, the larger the potential realized.

Spiritual Perspective:

Have you noticed that the most fascinating people are the ones who seem to create life around them? Have you also noticed that the people who are the most opinionated are usually the most interesting? That is because they are typically people who do not settle for anything less in life. It is always about achieving higher, doing more, and truly living life to the fullest.

Sometimes, these individuals intimidate us but they provide the truest example of authentic being and living. When you admire anything about another, you are admiring an aspect of your self. Once you believe this you may cultivate any aspect of yourself to something grander, and then you can take the first step toward embracing your potential. This is always about defining yourself toward something more sublime.

The most difficult part of change is allowing things to move into the past. This is not about who gets your old job or who is with your former love, this is about you shedding what no longer works toward revealing your best possible self. Find that emotion (even if it is tiny) that excites you about your life and cultivate that emotion. Let that spark propel you to your absolute best.

At some point, you must shine on your own.

Ritual:

On a slip of paper write the following affirmation: "My potential is constantly revealing itself to me and I am capable of action at the fortuitous moment."

THREE + THREE
LOVE
(supporting gem/mineral: platinum)

YES

Physical Plane:

Casting THREE + THREE indicates perfect balance for all things concerning your question. It is everything supporting your decision. There is no question that love flows through this query and that the Universe resounds affirmation. You can do nothing wrong now. Your confidence is high, the people involved love and support you and this moment of truth benefits all concerned. Yes, you will get the job, a soul connection, or a desired outcome. All shadows of doubt are eliminated by the brightness of the energy that is generated by your spirit.

Know that success is assured and act accordingly.

Spiritual Perspective:

Each lifetime, the Universe shifts and opens the way for us to fulfill our fondest dreams. This is that moment for you. Nothing but celebration of your spirit is called for now. You have worked to this moment to take advantage of something greater and more gratifying than anything you have experienced in this lifetime. There is only room in your heart for love and gratitude.

It will feel dizzying at times to see cherished goals realized and you will understand what all this hard work was about. Celebrate, and thank those who assisted you. You are ready; embrace the absolute greatness you deserve. There is no "payback" here; you are simply withdrawing from the Universe the energy that you have invested. This is truly an example of allowing yourself to enjoy what you have manifested.

You have learned to emphasize what is perfect and empowered about you. You are showing others, by your example, that they can realize anything you can visualize. It is your path and destiny to experience this intensity of excellence. You will eventually help others to learn to realize their dreams, but for now, enjoy and celebrate that your success is exactly what you have earned and deserve.

Splendor and light encourage your path.

Ritual:

On a slip of paper write the following affirmation: "Every event in my life has lead me to enjoy this time of success."

THREE + FOUR
RISK NOTHING
(supporting gem/mineral: turquoise)

NO

Physical Plane:

Rolling THREE + FOUR indicates that you will do well to take no risks or impulsive action at this time. This is about what others have to offer you, not what you have to offer them. There are times when we are asked to give something of value of our selves at no promise of a return-in-kind. This is not a good time to give away your time, talent, money or effort without some confirmation of a guaranteed return. This is also not a good time to change jobs or careers. This combination of dice asks you to be wary of people asking you to perform for them as an expectation.

Hold your gifts away from those who do not have the capacity to appreciate them.

Spiritual Perspective:

There are times when giving is all we know how to do. However, the Universe is showing you that you have been giving, producing, or spending too much. This is a time to realize that your unique gift to your world is being abused. You have sent out the message that somehow others are entitled to your gift. This is the time to retreat, recharge, and reexamine how much you might be exhausting.

This is not a good time for negotiating important contracts or court proceedings. The parties involved feel as though they are entitled to goodwill directly generated by you. This puts you at a disadvantage in any mediation process. While in retreat mode, consider those around you who offer something to their world that you consider valuable. Inspire yourself with biographies of people who have created successes in their lives.

Consider employing a skilled negotiator on your behalf to represent you in this matter. An attorney, agent, or recruiter will do far more for you than you can do on your own at this time. It may be time to enlist their expertise. Sometimes we can only go so far before we call in assistance toward reaching something important. An enlightened person knows when to ask for support.

The most accomplished people typically have the best team working on their behalf.

Ritual:

On a slip of paper write the following affirmation: "The correct individual or experience will help me realize what I deserve."

THREE + FIVE
TRUSTING POWER
(supporting gem/mineral: carnelian)

YES

Physical Plane:

Rolling THREE + FIVE asks you to recognize your personal power. You have probably experienced some difficulties in your past and few joys happened easily. This is the point when experiences in life bring you more joy. It is a time of trusting that you deserve the gifts that are currently presented. Gifts such as love, devotion, faith, opportunities, pleasure and abundance are now aspects of your reality. This trusting power allows you to believe in the splendor of life again. It is knowledge that divine timing is now working with you to reward you for all the work, energy and love you have given.

It is now time to live your dream.

Spiritual Perspective:

An enlightened being receives this combination only when they have full knowledge of the dark and the light of the world. They choose to close the door on what does not promote love, light and beauty in their lives. It is the simple act of ignoring negative influences by not allowing them power. There is no gripping emotion; this is an act of choice simply for the greater good and potential of their spirit.

Trust represents the highest personal freedom we can adopt. The simple act of choice will allow change in our lives in that moment. Each new life happens in a moment; whether it is conception of a child or the decision to make your life more fulfilled. This is very powerful for people who are curious about their purpose or meaning of life. Choice is one of our greatest gifts.

Typically, your meaning of life is that thing or activity in which you give the greatest share of time. Consider what deserves your attention. Is it something to celebrate or something you shame? Both are a choice, and in your case, you now have the strength to incorporate the most meaningful actions in your life. Trust that exactly the right situation will unfold for you at the moment it is required. This is where you learn about real happiness.

Have confidence on the path of your new, and more contented life.

Ritual:

On a slip of paper write the following: "I trust my progress."

THREE + SIX
COMPLETE DIRECTION
(supporting gem/mineral: kunzite)

NO

Physical Plane:

Casting THREE + SIX means that you are receiving clear direction toward your goal. Watch for opportunities that present themselves and take advantage of any offer or education that you possibly can. Although this means surety of your path, it does not present sweeping changes at this time. There is an area of study to contemplate or a step that must be taken to add credentials to your experience. However, you will encounter a vision of your aspiration ahead and success is assured. Develop relationships with people in key positions and perform the appropriate work.

Patience and purpose bring your goal to you.

Spiritual Perspective:

You possess the patience and maturity to finish the required tasks and then the realization of your goal. This will be a well-deserved celebration of hard work and persistence. There are no shortcuts and through this education, accreditation, project or physical effort, your success is imminent. Make sure there is time for you to acknowledge the small accomplishments along the way.

Productive patience is the most effective thought process right now. There are many events aligning themselves now for the arrival of your finished project. Keep yourself mentally, emotionally, spiritually, and physically balanced at this time. Develop friendships with those on the same journey, as they will be important to you in the future. Mostly, use this time to make sure that you are preparing for your personal achievement.

This combination frequently arises for the perpetual student. When you find yourself at a loss for what action to take, choosing the action that in some way prepares you for success will be satisfying in ways you cannot see now. Allowing room for your creative side to manifest at this time will help make this time of waiting more productive. There are times for action and times for productive waiting.

How you pass the time now will teach you how to pragmatically wait for what you want.

Ritual:

On a slip of paper write the following: "This time of alert patience and work (or study) is leading me directly to my goal."

Date	Question

Date	Question

FOUR

Four is the number of structure and resonates to the
word "Truth." This number is about practical
concerns and reflects the outward reality of
our inner vision.

Four represents the material.

FOUR + ONE
NEW IDEAS
(supporting gem/mineral: amethyst)

NO

Physical Plane:

Rolling FOUR + ONE tells you that it is time for new ideas. Your foundation is strong, however, it is important for you to obtain a fresh perspective. It is time to connect with new people and cultures. Artists, actors, and authors benefit from this dice combination, as it is the introduction of your muse. Gaining original and new ideas from contemporary sources truly benefits your question. Take yourself to any new creative experience, as it will open your mind to greater possibilities. Let yourself entertain the thought that the perfect idea will occur to you at precisely the right moment.

Greater possibilities happen when you are willing to change something.

Spiritual Perspective:

When we think that our way is the only way we block ourselves from the creative source. Even if you decide to try something different, it does not mean you have less credit or worth – it is still your idea. This is a good time for relaxed activity, meditation, automatic writing, and spiritual unity. Any way you can inspire yourself to try something new, it is important that you do so.

Plan a vacation where you are as close to nature as possible, someplace beautiful and serene. While on this trip, get involved with the local culture as much as possible. Attend the local theater; try new foods; and visit the places where the locals gather. While there, imagine that your every whim can be created in a moment. Delight in meeting and talking with the people. Write down every interaction and experience.

When you get back home, treat your neighborhood as though you were seeing it for the first time. What does it have; what do you think it needs; and how would you change it if you could? Once you take the idea of change outside of yourself, you can embrace the change within yourself. Just a small shift will be all it takes for your creative flow to begin anew.

Remember, it takes less than a moment for inspiration – prepare for it.

Ritual:

On a slip of paper write the following affirmation: "Divine inspiration flows effortlessly through to me."

FOUR + TWO
SELF-ACTUALIZATION
(supporting gem/mineral: clear quartz)

YES

Physical Plane:

Casting FOUR + TWO tells you that you have reached the pinnacle in regard to your question and success will reach many areas of your life. You have "arrived" and can now relax and enjoy the processes involved in completion. You possess self-acceptance to the level in which you feel "at home" wherever you are. There is no longer a desire to be anyone else but you. Everyone connected with you notices a difference about you although nothing really physical about you has changed. You are now allowing your most brilliant self to shine and doors are thrown open for you.

You now acknowledge how remarkable you are.

Spiritual Perspective:

Your intuition is accurate; others are responding to you; and your world is rewarding you in kind. This is the point we all strive to reach in our lifetime and it is always about a cherished goal or dream. It is a moment of omnipotence that will flow into many areas of your life.

Important knowledge is available to you just at the moment it is required. This is the prize for your focus and hard work.

If we take a moment to truly recognize our potential we can accomplish amazing leaps. This is the time where you understand just how a personal desire is rewarded at a soul level. It is an insight that every aspect of being comprehends; yet it is difficult to explain to another person. Even though focus and hard work have brought this moment to you it still feels miraculous.

You will find that future projects take on the flavor of success before any real planning commences. You have discovered that you are a creator. People are drawn to you now because they sense that unique quality that is entirely yours. This time is about relaxed focus and finishing touches. You have nothing but the highest level of excellence working with you now.

Your most unique and powerful self is recognized.

Ritual:

On a slip of paper write the following affirmation: "I am now realizing how my unique gifts benefit myself and everyone concerned."

FOUR + THREE
COINCIDENCE
(supporting gem/mineral: lapis lazuli)

NO

Physical Plane:

Rolling FOUR + THREE tells you that you are about to be presented with seemingly coincidental events. These events may be subtle or glaring but they have certainly been created to gain your attention. Thinking of someone and that person calls, encountering an old friend, or finding something that is the ideal fit for a project. Whatever the coincidence, it is working in your life for your benefit. This is the time of omens and signs with almost immediate results. Awareness in the moment is the most fortuitous attitude to adopt now. Miss nothing about people or surroundings.

Your encouragement will arrive through a coincidence.

Spiritual Perspective:

Though this is not a time of significant action, it will prompt action shortly. The Universe will provide you with a sign for a slight redirection of your plans. Simply, it is time to wait for what you know will be successful and also a time for you to be open enough to allow some pleasant surprises. Comfortable omens and people will provide you with what you require for action.

Chance meetings will prove to be very beneficial at this time because you will find more in common with others now. This is a good time for networking and socializing to increase your potential for meaningful connections. Attending a charitable event allows you to reach beyond your usual circle of people. New acquaintances will become cherished friends and business associates in the future.

Watch for a perfect feather in your path as it indicates something exciting and important is about to happen. This is an omen that you are exactly where you are supposed to be at that moment. If you find this feather on the way to a meeting, there will be something personally significant about to transpire. Pay attention to the messages being sent to you, these messages are beneficial to your goals.

Coincidence is working on your behalf.

Ritual:

On a slip of paper write the following affirmation: "I will recognize that helpful influences will appear as coincidences."

FOUR + FOUR
BALANCE

(supporting gem/mineral: silver)

YES

Physical Plane:

Rolling FOUR+ FOUR indicates that every facet of your character is in appropriate balance for success. This is the number of power, fate, and destiny; a combination of justice served and encouragement of action. You finally will begin to see the reward for your difficult journey and it is time to bless and release the past. You have experienced a more arduous journey in life than most, and it is time to recognize that this moment would not be as important to you if your past had been different. You now have the maturity, knowledge, and support to step into your power.

Divine power works through you now.

Spiritual Perspective:

Increased abundance is assured as long as you comprehend the power and responsibility associated with it. Most people simply think about the things they would have if they were wealthy; you have thought beyond physical possessions to sovereignty. Affluence represents autonomy and freedom to you, which is why is it of such significant importance. Your utmost goal now is acceptance and achievement of excellence.

This is the gentle balance of the inner and outer world. Any doubts regarding your progress are shadows of fear and only need be brought into light to dissolve. The balance of your spiritual growth only confirms that you only need imagine the highest good and abundance and the appropriate tools will be presented. Do not apologize anymore for your greatness; your life is all about you now.

As always, there will be distractions and those who criticize your focus and intent. Because balance is working for you now, you must embrace your right to be selfish enough to attain your goal. This time will provide a fresh perspective about others; if they cannot encourage (or tolerate) the good things that result from your effort and focused attention, then they will ultimately undermine you when your success is realized.

A strong sense of self and focus brings you great success.

Ritual:

On a slip of paper write the following affirmation: "It is my right to shine for all the gifts I possess with all the support and love available."

FOUR + FIVE
CREDIBILITY

(supporting gem/mineral: smoky quartz)

NO

Physical Plane:

Casting FOUR + FIVE represents your (or another's) claim of competency. There is proof and credibility to be provided in connection with your question. Whether you must provide proof of your accomplishments to someone or another is required to present them to you, it is of utmost importance that the qualifications be true, accurate, and timely. History and characteristics of major purchases must be explored. This is not a time to operate on trust or hearsay; you must perform the task to either provide required information to someone or have the person in question provide it to you.

Credibility will protect you now.

Spiritual Perspective:

When we get swept up in important projects, it is easy to miss crucial details. Because you are charting unknown territory now, fears will manifest at this time as details missed. You will avoid uncomfortable delays to your progress by making sure that every aspect around you is authentic. History supports you now as it reflects the appropriate potentials involved. Do not apologize or be threatened by this required information.

If angry emotions emerge as a result of attaining credibility, examination and pause are the actions required. If the information is provided effortlessly, then it is an indication to proceed. There will be public exam and celebration in connection with your question and like someone engaging in politics, make sure that every action is honorable and sincere.

Just like the preparation before a long journey; it is important that all the items you take are clean and in good working order. This is not a time to give someone a "second chance" or assist someone who has yet to prove their worth. You are presented with the power and value of credibility as a sign that this time indicates a final test for you to alleviate your fear of success.

Celebrate that you understand the worth of genuine accomplishment.

Ritual:

On a slip of paper write the following affirmation: "My credibility is valuable and important and others readily provide theirs."

FOUR + SIX
LUCK
(supporting gem/mineral: jade)

YES

Physical Plane:

Rolling the combination FOUR + SIX represents how luck applies in your life. Examine whether you attract "good" or "bad" luck and modify your perspective accordingly. Though this number sequence frequently resonates with gamblers, inventors, and investors, it also applies to those successful individuals who have taken large risks or leaps in life. These powerful individuals rarely dwell on negative past experiences and typically view themselves as fortunate and positive. You are exactly where you must be to experience success and good fortune.

Decide that you are lucky and you will be.

Spiritual Perspective:

We create our own luck by deciding where we want to be in life and pursuing those goals. True luck is about the energy we create in and around us. It is about being prepared at all times for the perfect opportunity, whether that is looking your physical best during a "chance" meeting or having your credentials available at the time they are requested.

If you think the world is against you and nothing good happens in your life then you are right. If instead, you realize that you have exactly the tools in any moment to make your life more joyous and purposeful, then you have changed your luck. People do not win major contracts, radiant health, or jackpots unless somewhere within themselves they believe they deserve them.

Lady Luck is not fickle; she is instead seeking worthy companionship. Doubt is your biggest enemy now and while it is not recommended that you "bet the farm," it is suggested that you open your mind to the idea that the Universe is always supporting you to live the happiest life you can imagine. Once you can comprehend that real luck is about opening your heart to love then, you can have anything you want.

The more love in our heart, the greater the luck in our lives.

Ritual:

On a slip of paper write the following affirmation: "I am at all times blessed, loved and lucky."

Date	Question

Date	Question

FIVE

Five is the number of communication at all levels and represents the word "Engagement." This is the message sent to the Universe and your commitment.

Five is the number of thought.

FIVE + ONE
REPUTATION

(supporting gem/mineral: aquamarine)

YES

Physical Plane:

Casting FIVE + ONE represents your public image. This is where you will decide (now and in the future) how you will be perceived in your environment. An important aspect of reputation is the value of your word. Do you keep your promises to people? This is not about how others respond to you; this is how you respond to others. People are counting on you to keep your agreements. As your individual power increases, be judicious and discerning with your word. Others are holding you responsible for the honor of your pledge and it is wise to be conscientious.

Your reputation will pave the way for you.

Spiritual Perspective:

Your responsibility to yourself and then to others does not end while you are still learning in the physical world. The correct order of things is first to embrace and realize your potential and then decide on the people you will help along the way. It is always better to experience personal success on an individual level before partnering with anyone else. This applies to both personal and business unions.

Without a strong sense of accomplishment and self, you become someone who follows the ideas of another. While there is some comfort in surrendering your potential, you will eventually find an undercurrent of dissatisfaction in your situation. Gradually, the things that provided satisfaction no longer do so. If these words sting a bit, then you are being directed to find something within so you can shine on your own.

Your greatness will attract people who have not worked as diligently as you and will attempt to take advantage of your current good nature. They will ask you for favors with no promise of reciprocity; avoid these people, as they do not truly value your effort. You have a noteworthy talent and the Universe is poised to reward you. This is the result of realizing your potential and the hard work it has taken to get to this place.

Learn to evaluate others in a graciously perceptive manner.

Ritual:

On a slip of paper write the following affirmation: "Time and my word are valued treasures and I know who is worthy of these gifts."

FIVE + TWO
MENTOR
(supporting gem/mineral: hematite)

NO

Physical Plane:

Casting FIVE + TWO assists you in realizing your inner and outer mentors. This is a time of self-discovery and self-awareness. It is a good time to test your aptitude and perhaps develop one of your natural gifts. Your intuition will be sharply tuned toward those signals and people who act as a teacher in some way in regard to your question. Pay particular attention to psychic impressions, dreams, and secret information. A strong sense of purpose and meaning is about to be recognized. Stay grounded through routine in the physical dynamics of your day, as personal breakthroughs are powerful.

You are the champion of the meaning of your life.

Spiritual Perspective:

Whatever empowers you spiritually will help to ground you through this important self-discovery. Whether your outward life is calm or in turmoil, it is essential that your personal philosophy be established or strengthened. Ultimately, everything turns out perfectly for the purpose in our life, however, sometimes we mentally stray or are oblivious to our goals while in physical form.

When we realize that everything around us began as a thought somewhere, we realize just how much energy we possess. Your life can and will change in a moment. A personal example of this is on the horizon for you. This is why it is vital that you recognize where you draw your strength. This will be your sanctuary and power source for all the events that will begin shortly in your life.

Why do you work the way you do? What drives you? Are you living up to your expectations of this lifetime? These are the questions to begin with. This moment is about you and the lessons you are realizing now that are important. It does not matter what you consider your motivation for success and self-actualization, it is only essential that you become greater than you are now.

The depth of your personal potential and scope is astonishing.

Ritual:

On a slip of paper write the following affirmation: "Significant events unfold for me to discover my true-place purpose and path."

FIVE + THREE
VICTORY

(supporting gem/mineral: tiger eye)

YES

Physical Plane:

Rolling FIVE + THREE assures victory of your question, situation or concern. Health matters will attract the correct energy for healing; a promotion in your career is certain; or you are about to appreciate a greater understanding of real unconditional love. Fairness reigns and court cases are judged in your favor. This is an especially fortuitous combination for any question concerning a desired goal, opportunity, or outcome. All parties concerned support your victory and progress. This is an excellent time to launch a new project or business.

The Universe nods her head in your favor.

Spiritual Perspective:

You are being collectively rewarded for your hard work and effort even if this seems to have come to you easily. It is your lesson to accept this gift presented with loving thoughts of gratitude. This combination only arises when someone has earned the right to be "the best" or "expert" in some fashion. You are being universally recognized and acknowledged.

Sometimes, it is just as uncomfortable to accept acclaim, as it is to tolerate criticism. The scales have tipped to allow you the adventure of a buoyant and uplifting experience. This is the pinnacle of your journey for now and it is your right to enjoy this attention. There will be an opportunity for you to allow another to shine in the future, but for now, it is your turn.

Document and celebrate this time for your future reference and write about all the emotions this event has revealed. You have been given the gift of festivity after a significant amount of focus and hard work. If this occasion seems to have arrived easily then it indicates that you have found a purposeful life and success in this arena was destined to happen before you take your next big step.

Celebration of purpose is revealed to you now.

Ritual:

On a slip of paper write the following affirmation: "I embrace all the rewards of the Universe."

FIVE + FOUR
CHARITY
(supporting gem/mineral: moonstone)

NO

Physical Plane:

Producing FIVE + FOUR in a roll asks you to consider those people whose lives are not as abundant as yours. Your life has reached a plateau or a standstill in some way and a heartfelt, earnest gesture of generosity will help things to flow again. This is about you giving the gift of your time, word, or abundance in a direction where it is sincerely appreciated. Even a small contribution to a charitable organization will help you break the stagnation that has developed in your life at this time. Giving now places you back in the perspective of power.

Outward flow of abundance (power) releases stagnation and blockage.

Spiritual Perspective:

Sometimes this combination is cast when you are asked to give up something really valuable for your life to progress. The more you believe that the Universe will always provide you with the gift of abundance, then the perceived taking away or giving of things is only a mental attitude. However, this perspective will ultimately affect all aspects of our lives, especially money.

When you hold on to anything too tightly, it will lose its original form and appeal. You become imprisoned or even obsessed by it and no longer have the freedom you enjoyed when you first attained it. The giving of something greatly valued to another who shows gratitude and appreciation provides you with a very powerful perspective. The freedom to not be owned by a "thing."

Think of the people who buy a very expensive automobile and are not in the mind-set of abundance to appreciate it. They are compulsive about every potential scratch or ding, the road they drive, and the parking places they select. It's not about the enjoyment of a beautiful and functional vehicle anymore; it is about their using the item to create an identity. That is not true abundance; it is only materialism.

The Universe supports both our dynamic and receptive natures – choose dynamic.

Ritual:

Write the following affirmation on a slip of paper: "Thoughtful gifts of time and abundance create flow."

FIVE + FIVE
TRUTH/TRUST
(*supporting gem/mineral: peridot*)

YES

Physical Plane:

Rolling FIVE + FIVE tells you that you have arrived at the moment of truth. There are no deceptions now and you have the appropriate knowledge to proceed. This combination celebrates true-place success or a step in that particular direction. You are required now to live your truth and love at the greatest capacity. You may trust the parties involved, the businesses in question or the person of your desire. Nothing will hold you back now if you trust that each step will alight just at the moment you require it. This is your moment to seize.

Universal and divine timing is now.

Spiritual Perspective:

The Universe is providing you with the ideal situation to trust. Mostly, this combination arises when you are required to trust your-self, however, this may also mean that you are asked to trust another person. It is still supported, even with the doubts that may arise. You might be saying hello or good-bye to someone important and cherished. It is important that you trust enough to take the implied action or step.

Typically, when you are asked to trust another it is when your life is at a turning point. It may be that they are beginning or changing their life in some significant way. Trust that however you assist that person in attaining their dream, you will always be rewarded in some fashion, even if you do not personally discover the result of your contribution. This time of trust has farther-reaching effects than you expect.

You may be asked to lead a new project or take on a job you have never done before. Is it finally time to begin your own business; move someplace beautiful; or give your heart to another? Now is the time. The more you trust now, the more love you will experience in your life. The power in this time of trust is invigorating; know that each element of your path is such that you can trust with an open and expectant heart.

Great things bloom out of a simple truth.

Ritual:

On a slip of paper write the following affirmation: "I trust my true progress and potential without reserve."

FIVE + SIX
VISUALIZATION
(supporting gem/mineral: amethyst)

NO

Physical Plane:

Casting FIVE + SIX signifies that you must have a clear picture of what you wish in your mind's eye. Imagining that you are already in the career you desire; the relationship you want; and the affluence you deserve. This is a powerful combination that supports your ultimate dreams. Your mind must be engaged and convinced that what you seek is already a comfortable aspect of your life. This is why some people place a photo of the object or vacation spot they wish to have so the mind can capture it. The clearer your picture, the more likely you will bring that reality into your life.

The more vibrant your visualization, the quicker it will manifest.

Spiritual Perspective:

Our mind knows little difference between waking and sleeping. It experiences both with the same emotional and mental engagement. Our dreams, however, allow us to delve into areas not permissible in our current material, Earth plane state. We can break rules and live our multiple fantasies. Lucid dreamers are able to direct their dreaming state toward adventures and obtain answers to perplexing problems.

Visualization asks you to stretch your mind into a great expansive scope. Decide that wealth is much more than the amount of your paycheck. Instead, imagine a way of life where choice, comfort, love, and contentment are a natural experience of your day. Look forward to the moment where you relive the adventure of this moment and how your mind grasped and created a greater and more fulfilling reality.

Your story is always about how you aligned yourself with your greatest and most authentic self. Each lifetime, we decide how much we will suffer or celebrate that life. The most genuine life embodies compassion, capacity, and comprehension. It is the journey and the ever-changing destinations of that journey. Your potential is unique and precious and you are the one who determines your life.

Dream larger than you have ever dared and grasp your potential completely.

Ritual:

On a slip of paper write the following affirmation: "When I can imagine it in my life, it will soon be a real part of my life."

Date	Question

Date	Question

SIX

Six is the number of consideration and represents the word "Love." It is the number that most represents living one's true nature where compassion is always in deed.

Six is the number of passion.

SIX + ONE
CONNECTED

(supporting gem/mineral: celestite)

NO

Physical Plane:

Rolling SIX + ONE asks you to pay close attention to how things are connected together, how things relate to each other, and the atmosphere of your question. This combination indicates that there is a greater issue connected with this question and you have only a glimpse of the bigger picture at this time. This issue may or may not be known to you, however it is important to the outcome. Others are affected by this matter and you cannot proceed until you connect with everyone concerned. Keep an open mind to the energy around you today; the answer will come through an unexpected resource.

The impact of what you propose to do is bigger than you can grasp now.

Spiritual Perspective:

There are no accidents. Every moment or event in your life has directed you to this question and you were not ready to ask it until now. Your emotional state, your wisdom, and your preparedness have brought you to this current situation. You are being asked to consider your place in the Universe and how it all interrelates around you. You are at a sacred place now in your heart and in your life.

This is the brink of enlightenment, the understanding that your presence on this Earth is as precious as every other element of Her. Consider celebrating the divine timing of all things and the patient, almost amused assurance of your chosen path. You are given a moment of excited anticipation that something astonishing is about to be born. The greatest achievements arrive once we realize the purpose of our lives.

Acknowledge the people you admire with the silent recognition that they too, have been at this exact point at some time in their lives. The instant before the acclaim, success, and understanding are the powerful reasons we have chosen to live in human form. Then, think of all the people who have assisted you to reach this time in your life and send them their deserved admiration in your heart.

You have always directed the abundant energy of your intent; now it manifests.

Ritual:

Write the following affirmation on a slip of paper: "I now have the capacity to appreciate all the circumstances that brought me here."

SIX + TWO
LUST/STRENGTH
(supporting gem/mineral: ruby)

YES

Physical Plane:

Casting SIX + TWO asks you to contemplate how you support the energy of yearning in your life. Consider how much the subject of your question is worth to you. Is it worth concentration beyond all other things? Approach this issue as if you are courting and coaxing your goal, not aggravating it. Be aware of your pursuit and the signs that present themselves, but also be somewhat aloof to the conclusion. Behave in each interaction as though you are expecting the most favorable result. This attitude will serve you to negotiate most interactions.

You can give yourself permission to have what you want.

Spiritual Perspective:

The greatest energy given to most living creatures is sexual. The innate yearning to connect on the most intimate physical level is a part of the human experience. It is the closest and most basic physical reminder of love. It is also often misunderstood between men and women, yet it reflects the perfect balance of the masculine and feminine. The most satisfying expression of lust is the dance of give and take.

In classic ballroom dancing, you can watch the beauty of two beings delighting in the method and flow of their movement. There is no struggle between the two dancers engaged; instead, it appears as an effortless, silent communication of dynamic and surrender. That is the true expression of strength, the knowledge of the dance of the two opposites.

You are asked to recognize all the opposing aspects of your environment because if it were not for that tension, there would be no dance. Remember, the planets and stars in our solar system conduct the divine ballet of magnetism. It is as ancient as time and yet as wondrous as first love. Flirt with life again. Regardless of your physical age, remember that your spirit is young, splendid and divine.

You are ready to engage yourself again in the dance.

Ritual:

On a slip of paper write the following affirmation: "I am now dancing with all of life and look forward to my next engaging opportunity."

SIX + THREE
AUTONOMY

(supporting gem/mineral: blue sapphire)

NO

Physical Plane:

Rolling SIX + THREE tells you that it is time to operate autonomously on your concern. You already know what you are going to do and this dice casting simply confirms that action. This is the time to celebrate that you are doing the right thing, pursuing the right avenue, and possess perfect timing. Keep your decision to yourself until after you have acted on the matter. There is power in confidence and this is not the time to discuss your proposed actions with others. You will know what to do at the precise moment that you will feel obliged to act.

This is the time to trust your Higher Self.

Spiritual Perspective:

At some point in our lives, we will learn to trust that we know the correct thought, word or deed. We will see it in others and acknowledge it within. Not only is this about recognizing that we will be able to tackle whatever we are dealt, it is also seeing in others that same capacity. This is called the power of "I" and is the most evocative recognition we can embrace in our lives.

Acknowledgement of "I" is the first step toward self-actualization. It is the unique expression of your most enlightened and magnificent Self. We are not at the whim of some fate or destiny that is beyond us or outside of us. We are simply aligning ourselves with the path we chose before incarnation into this lifetime. This puts our power back where it belongs – our perfect omnipotent Spirit–Self directing our mundane human self.

It is both empowering and frightening to be yourself. Most people are the sum total of others' opinions. At some point when we begin to realize that it is much more challenging to live up to our own expectations, because innately we know our capacity. Life is magical because we have the power of choice, the power of self-awareness and the gift of this life.

You are at the age of reason – decide on your gift.

Ritual:

On a slip of paper write the following affirmation: "I now have the energy, intelligence, and ability to decide the right action."

SIX + FOUR
FORTUNE/CHANGE
(supporting gem/mineral: labradorite)

YES

Physical Plane:

Rolling SIX + FOUR asks you to make a friend of change because it is about to make a friend of you. The more disruptive and sweeping the change the better it will be for you. This combination indicates a benevolent set of circumstances and you will be ready to take advantage of the moment. You will have the resources, the right situation, and the right person will be there when you need them. You can now realize that you can have what you want. Say yes and celebrate your good fortune. Give yourself permission to move forward because the luck of preparation meeting opportunity has merged.

You are supported in every aspect.

Spiritual Perspective:

Although to others it may appear as if this was an effortless turn of fortune on your behalf, it is actually the result of your hard work and diligence. It is also your spirit's recognition that each life is filled with endings and beginnings. You are about to begin a new cycle of your life and in that is all the excitement of living the new experience. Bless and appreciate all the people and circumstances that brought you to this moment.

The most impressive achievement we can witness in our lifetime is something we thought about internally being manifested externally. Whether it is someone to love, a dream opportunity, or simply doing what feels both challenging and rewarding, it is all a result of what we believe we have the capacity to embrace. Allow yourself to enjoy this moment of recognition of your true Self-potential.

Once you open your mind to the concept that most changes are working for our highest good and potential, you will find yourself on an accelerated momentum. Others who operate on a higher vibration will subconsciously acknowledge you as a person of influence. You will draw to you supportive and meaningful people. Be prepared to accept the responsibility of a person of abundance.

All is aligning for you to succeed.

Ritual:

On a slip of paper write the following affirmation: "My focus and hard work now manifest my fortune and prosperity."

SIX + FIVE
DESTINY

(supporting gem/mineral: iolite)

NO

Physical Plane:

Rolling SIX + FIVE tells you that fate, karma, and destiny are supporting your every action now. Though this casting supports action soon in relation to your question, it actually is more a time of questioning all the events that have brought you to this moment. You are about to enjoy the swing of circumstances in your favor and it is timely to prepare for that change. Study every communication coming toward you now with the perspective of preparing for action. One of the items you receive will grant you clear indication of timing.

You are patiently awaiting your call to action.

Spiritual Perspective:

This combination typically appears when you are ready to move forward yet circumstances seem to be working against you. It is very important that you allow yourself permission to tackle the test of waiting and do nothing that works against your progress. The moment to take action will be so obvious that there will be no question about the timing to act.

In your divine state, you have chosen this moment. This time represents great potential when your energies and the energies around you have formed critical mass. Something magnificent is about to be born and your mundane human self cannot rush the process. Simply allow this opportunity to unfold with the patient expectancy of something superb. Hold confidence that all your challenges and focus are about to be rewarded.

Consider how your environment must change to accommodate your new way of life and prepare for that change as you wait. You won't have time to attend to all the small things once your door opens for you. Connect with all of the people who have supported you through all of your challenges and let them know you are expecting something big any moment. Enjoy the anticipation of something great developing for you.

Watch the Universe unfold for you.

Ritual:

On a slip of paper write the following affirmation: "It is easy to wait for my magnificent and brilliant adventure to begin."

SIX + SIX
ALL
(supporting gem/mineral: diamond)

YES

Physical Plane:

Rolling SIX + SIX tells you that your path is open to what you seek to achieve. The work is joyful, the events memorable, and the people involved are working with clear heart and focus. You cannot even ruin this moment. Your hard work and single-mindedness now allow you success, prosperity, abundance, and most of all the understanding of the significance of love. This is the realization of your potential, the understanding of your place in this world and the assurances that your life will never be the same. You have touched the sublime.

All that you seek to have in your life is at your fingertips now.

Spiritual Perspective:

This moment is the realization of why you were born into this lifetime. It is the identification of your purpose, the understanding of the power of love, and the result of living your life to its highest potential. The external around you is reflecting what your mind has embraced. This is the most powerful and fortunate combination of all the combinations.

Celebrate all of those individuals who showed you the Universe was moving through them to help you; even those people who made you upset or appeared to be working against you. All the aspects that occurred to bring you to this place had to be there for you to succeed and realize this moment. Allow yourself to appreciate just how much you are loved because you chose to love everything about your life.

This cycle places you in a position to assist someone else and in doing so you help him or her realize his or her chosen destiny. Since you now understand that you had to recognize and act upon your unique gift first before you could be of any assistance to someone else, the power behind your gift of assistance is now genuine. By your achievement through what you love, you can now recognize the true potential of another.

You have earned this pinnacle, now, what is the next one?

Ritual:

Write the following affirmation on a slip of paper: "I have the ability and resources to manifest all that my mind's eye can envision."

Date	Question

Date	Question

Appendix

Word Key for Dice Combinations

1.   One + One = Divine Agreement   (gold)

2.   One + Two = Gathering   (yellow topaz)

3.   One + Three = Priorities   (moldavite)

4.   One + Four = Foundation   (black tourmaline)

5.   One + Five = Intention   (citrine)

6.   One + Six = Release   (topaz)

7.   Two + One = Gratitude   (amber)

8.   Two + Two = Friendship   (emerald)

9.   Two + Three = Unity   (obsidian)

10. Two + Four = Kindness   (garnet)

11. Two + Five = Credible Witness   (pyrite)

12. Two + Six = Soul Mate Connection   (rose quartz)

13. Three + One = Reflection   (pearl)

14. Three + Two = Potential   (opal)

15. Three + Three = Love   (platinum)

16. Three + Four = Risk Nothing   (turquoise)

17. Three + Five = Trusting Power   (carnelian)

18. Three + Six = Complete Direction   (kunzite)

19. Four + One = New Ideas   (amethyst)

20. Four + Two = Self-Actualization   (clear quartz)

21. Four + Three = Coincidence   (lapis lazuli)

22. Four + Four = Balance   (silver)

23. Four + Five = Credibility   (smoky quartz)

24. Four + Six = Luck   (jade)

25. Five + One = Reputation   (aquamarine)

26. Five + Two = Mentor   (hematite)

27. Five + Three = Victory   (tiger eye)

28. Five + Four = Charity   (moonstone)

29. Five + Five = Truth/Trust   (peridot)

30. Five + Six = Visualization   (amethyst)

31. Six + One = Connection   (celestite)

32. Six + Two = Desire/Strength   (ruby)

33. Six + Three = Autonomy   (blue sapphire)

34. Six + Four = Fortune/Change   (labradorite)

35. Six + Five = Destiny   (iolite)

36. Six + Six = All   (diamond)

Preparing Your Home for a New Beginning

How do you prepare your home for a new beginning? I wanted to share a simple do-it-yourself home cleansing ritual. Simply follow the steps below and you will have the advantage of all the best the Universe may offer. You may also repeat this ritual for the following events: New Year's Day; at the end of a relationship; at the beginning of a new job; after really negative people have left your house; or the morning of your birthday. This is also a good ritual if you are seeking to sell your home. This is a harmless way to create the best energy possible where you live.

1. Purchase some dried sage and cedar (with mini-charcoal burning disks) or a cedar burning stick and a container of sea salt or kosher salt. Wild Oats and Whole Foods carry these items, so do most metaphysical bookstores. Sage and cedar represent the balance of masculine and feminine energies.

2. Go through your home and remove any plants that are not thriving, clothes that do not fit, anything broken, and items that remind you of negative or depressing experiences from the past.

3. When you awaken on "This Day of New Beginnings," take a salt bath (one cup salt to a tub of water). After five minutes of soaking, lather up as usual, finish your normal grooming routine, dry off with a freshly laundered towel, and get dressed in freshly laundered clothing.

4. Wrap a small plate with foil and place the charcoal disk in the center of the plate. Light the charcoal disk and wait for about 30 seconds until the entire disk is smoldering. Sprinkle some sage and

cedar on the disk until it begins to smoke*. Keep some extra sage and cedar in a small bowl to keep the smoke going until the ritual is completed. (If you're using a smudge stick, follow the instructions on the stick until it begins to smoke.)

5. Beginning at your front door, make a counterclockwise circle around the perimeter of the door with your smoking sage and cedar. Then going to your left, (again counterclockwise) walk the entire inside perimeter of your house. (If your house is two-stories or more, begin at the floor where your front door is located and then go up and circle each next floor counterclockwise. If there is a floor above and below the level of your front door, do the main level first, then the next level up and then the level below the main entrance.) This counterclockwise circle releases any negative energy in the home.

6. Once you are back at the front door, still keeping the sage and cedar smoking, direct the smoke in a clockwise circle around the perimeter of your front door. Then turning to your right (clockwise), walk the entire inside of your home again. When you're back at the front door, do one more clockwise circle of the front door. The clockwise circle seals in positive energy.

7. Then go to the kitchen and pour water on the burning charcoal disk, smudge stick, or incense to make sure it's no longer a fire hazard before you throw it away. Open every window in your home and turn on the fans for about 5 minutes. That will clear out the smoke and bring all fresh new air into your house. (It also gets rid of that "sort of smells like marijuana" scent for which sage and cedar gets a bad rap.)

8. While the house is airing out, go to your freezer and dump out all the ice into your sink.

9. Close all your windows and turn off the fans. Your house is now

ready for a new beginning.

10. If you are performing this ritual on New Year's Day, have the following four items at the same meal before midnight:

a. Black-eyed peas – this is for luck in the New Year.

b. Some sort of leafy vegetable: spinach, collards or even lettuce – this is for money in the New Year.

c. Meat from an animal that doesn't scratch backward (chicken and turkeys scratch backward): pork is a good choice – this is so you don't go hungry in the New Year.

d. Something sweet: cookies, candy, cake, or ice cream – so you can count on sweet surprises in the New Year.

e. Lastly, be with someone you love (or really like) on New Year's Day. Who you are with on the first day of the year sets the tone for what you'll tolerate or celebrate for the entire year.

*If you think the burning smoke might trip a smoke detector, it's okay to open a few windows as you go around the house. You don't need a lot of smoke to accomplish this cleansing task.

Acknowledgements

In every endeavor, there are always people to thank and appreciate. The evolution process for me to become "Las Vegas' own Mystic Mona" has been one of the most wonderful adventures of this lifetime.

In one moment, anyone's life can change - "A shift in the Universe," as Meg would say. For me, it was the first time I had done (now memorable) Tarot readings for a group of Las Vegas friends after a hearty St. Patrick's dinner. It was such a wonderful evening, that it got me thinking that Las Vegas needs a good psychic. Sincere gratitude to those treasured individuals who were there: Sarah, Gordon, Deanna and Doug (the "DFs"), Bonnie and Doug, and my fabulous husband, Chuck.

Las Vegas requires a background investigation to be granted the Psychic Arts License. I appreciate those helpful people through **The City of Las Vegas and Las Vegas Metro** for guiding me through the entire licensing process. I commend my fellow psychics in Las Vegas who are also licensed and qualified.

Grateful thanks to **Kim McCabe** for having the faith to book me for my first major event at The Venetian Hotel and Casino and to **Deanna Forbush** for her introductions that first year. To **Fred Walters, David Watts, and Dawn Britt** of the Venetian's Grand Canal Shoppes for their professionalism and creativity.

Rikki Cheese (now an anchor on Channel 13) allowed fellow psychic, **Matthew Name** and me our radio debut on **88.1FM**. That gave me enough confidence to launch my radio show, Psychic View, on **970AM, KNEWS**. I'd like to thank **Andy Vierra** and **Ryan Smart**, for their expertise in helping me to develop my show and allowing me to be a guest during the afternoon drive.

Requiring additional program time, I consulted with **Gavin Spittle** and moved the show to **Infinity's Hottalk 1140, KSFN**. With the help of **Scott Delk** and **Jim McCarthy**, Psychic View is now the most popular show of its kind in Las Vegas. Thank you to the entertaining and spontaneous professionals of the **Johnson and Tofte Show,** as well as **The John David Wells Show** for featuring me on their programs.

Of course, I could not have a quality radio program if it were not for the sponsors of Psychic View. I am blessed with the resources and friendship from the following brilliant individuals who have contributed as past or current sponsors of my show: **Sarah Waghorn, Dr. Byron Blasco, Gilbert Niimi, Jack Woodcock, Scott Messinger, and Mike Randall** - their faith in me has been an inspiration.

To my radio friends who, by their example, make Las Vegas a better place: **Gena Satori with ReVamp Radio, Lark Williams with 97.1, The Point,** and **Thom Kaufold with XM NASCAR Radio.**

Thanks to the wonderful writers, editors and publishers of the Las Vegas Weekly for the continued support of the Psychic View column; especially, the creative columnist and contributing editor **Steve Bornfeld,** the witty managing editor, **Scott Dickensheets**, and publisher, **Pat Kelly.**

My weekly appearances on **FOX 5 News This Morning with** **Josh Talkington** and **Cher Calvin** were absolutely enjoyable. Thanks to all the **Fox 5** professionals, especially **Sabrina Brummond** and **Susan Lucas** for a mutually beneficial and wonderful morning feature.

To **Steve Bornfeld** for the editing of this book, and to the talented **Amber Mayes (ambermaze@aol.com)** for cover design, formatting, and printing consultation. **Chuck Joseph** is responsible for taking the great cover picture.

To **Bill** and **Petra of Frogparade.com** for their creation, suggestions, and on-going support of my website.

Especially Meaningful People:

Bonnie and Doug for being first and lasting friends in Las Vegas.

Sarah for being the most unforgettable person I know.

Trish and Spencer for kicking Sunday Dinner up a notch.

Sidra K. for being the best "boss" ever!

Sherry F. for her insight and humor.

Meg G. for the realization of my shift in the Universe.

Donna and Terralyn for those Friday nights.

Sherry D. and Arlinda for demonstrating the true power of love and free will.

Norman W. for the precious gift of his friendship.

Lisa M. for demonstrating unconditional love.

Yvonne S. for being the best human example of spiritual enlightenment that I know.

Barbara O. for her friendship during the formative years.

Beth C. for the longtime history of being my most treasured friend.

Mom & Dad for all the reasons.

To my fabulous husband, **Chuck**, because true love really is liberating and empowering.

Chancing Life

Give the gift of Chancing Life: Wisdom in a Dice Roll to your friends and colleagues.

Check your local bookstores or order here!

___YES! I want ____ copies of Chancing Life: Wisdom in a Dice Roll for $19.99 each.

____YES! I am interested in Mona Van Joseph as a speaker or to entertain as Mystic Mona for my guests at a special event. Please send me information.

Include $3.95 shipping and handling for one book, and $1.95 for each additional book. Nevada Residents please add 7.5% sales tax. Payment must accompany orders. Please allow three weeks for delivery.

My check or money order for $_____ is enclosed. Please make your check or money order payable in US funds to Mystic Ventures, Inc.

Name: (first)_____ (last) _____

Title:_____

Company:_____

Address:_____

City/State:_____ Zip:_____

Phone: _____

E-mail Address: _____

Credit Card Number: _____

Expiration Date: _____

Please circle one: American Express   Visa   Mastercard

Name on Credit Card: _____

Signature of Card Holder: _____

Mail orders to: Mystic Ventures, Inc.
9360 W. Flamingo Road, Suite 110-143, Las Vegas, NV 89147
(702) 571-0461 • www.chancinglife.com